The Little Book

About

BIG

Words

James Roberts

(Gentleman Jim)

The Little Book about BIG Words

James Roberts
(Gentleman Jim)

Many people were at the station, waiting for the train.
Do you know a **BIG** word for train?

Locomotive.

Can you say locomotive?
Lo-co-mo-tive. Good job!

Little Susie was very hungry for breakfast.
Do you know a **BIG** word for hungry?

Famished.

Can you say Famished?
Fam-ish-ed. Good job!

Little Bobby was sad when he couldn't find his toy.
Do you know a **BIG** word for sad?

Melancholy.

Can you say melancholy?
Mel-an-cho-ly. Good job!

Billy's room was very messy
Do you know a **BIG** word for messy?

Cluttered.

Can you say cluttered?
Clut-ter-ed. Good job!

Mom drove the kids to school in their car.
Do you know a **BIG** word for car?

Automobile.

Can you say automobile?
Au-to-mo-bile. Good job!

Tommy was in trouble for telling a lie.
Do you know a **BIG** word for lie?

Fabrication.

Can you say fabrication?
Fa-bri-ca-tion. Good job!

The teacher was showing the kids how to add.
Do you know a **BIG** word for add?

Calculate.

Can you say calculate?
Cal-cu-late. Good job!

They tried to fool the kids with the non-fruits drinks.
Do you know a **BIG** word for fool?

Bamboozle.

Can you say Bamboozle?
Bam-boo-zle. Good job!

Physician.

Can you say physician?
Phys-i-cian. Good job!

Mommy used fake sugar in her coffee.
Do you know a **BIG** word for fake?

Artificial.

Can you say artificial?
Ar-ti-fi-cial. Good job!

Susie wanted to make a new friend at the park.
Do you know a **BIG** word for friend?

Acquaintance.

Can you say acquaintance?
Ac-quain-tance. Good job!

Wow! Look at all the BIG words you've learned!

Locomotive
Famished
Melancholy
Cluttered
Automobile
Fabrication

Calculate
Bamboozle
Physician
Artificial
Acquaintance

Great job!!

Now
let's try
some fun
activities!!

WHICH ONE IS A LOCOMOTIVE?

WHICH KID IS FAMISHED?

WHICH KID IS MELANCHOLY?

WHICH TABLE IS CLUTTERED?

WHICH ONE IS AN AUTOMOBILE?

WHOSE STORY WAS A FABRICATION?

WHICH KID IS READY TO CALCULATE?

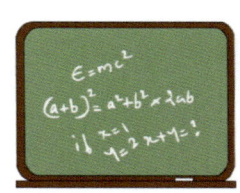

WHICH KID DID THE PARENTS BAMBOOZLE?

WHICH ONE IS A PHYSICIAN?

WHICH PERSON IS ARTIFICIAL?

WHICH KID HAS A NEW ACQUAINTANCE?

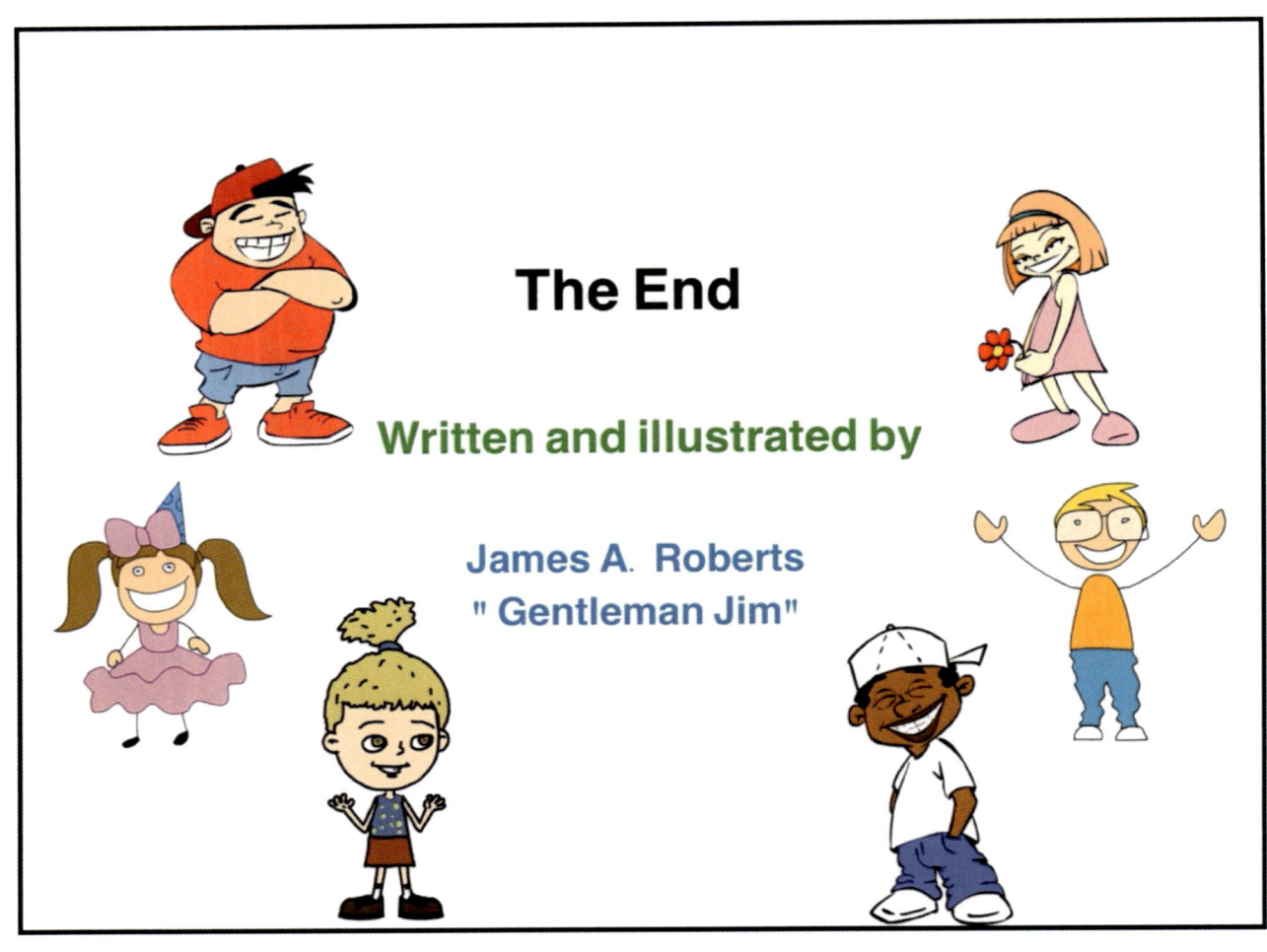

The End

Written and illustrated by

James A. Roberts
" Gentleman Jim"

This story created using an Ipad
The "Comics Head" storyboard app
and imagination

Special thanks to Brenda Van Niekerk
For formatting this story for Ebook publication

(Brenda@triomarketers. com)

Art by Comics Head
This book was made using Comics Head
The story telling app for apple and android
Art used by permission

Be on the lookout!!

Coming soon. . . . . . . **!!!!**

Another Little BOOK About BIG Words

By James Roberts
(Gentleman Jim)

Other books by Gentleman Jim:

The Little Book About BIG Words 1-6

The Little Book About FUN Words 1 and 2

The Thrill Seekers

The Little Book of Sayings

If you enjoyed this book, help spread the word!

*Like our Facebook page: The Little Book About BIG Words

*Follow us on Instagram: authorgentlemanjim

*Visit our website: Authorgentlemanjim.com

Or consider taking a moment and writing a review for us at Amazon.com or Goodreads.com

Thank You!!

Made in the USA
Columbia, SC
17 September 2020